Zoom in on
POWER GRIDS

Kathy Furgang

E **Enslow Publishing**
101 W. 23rd Street
Suite 240
New York, NY 10011
USA

enslow.com

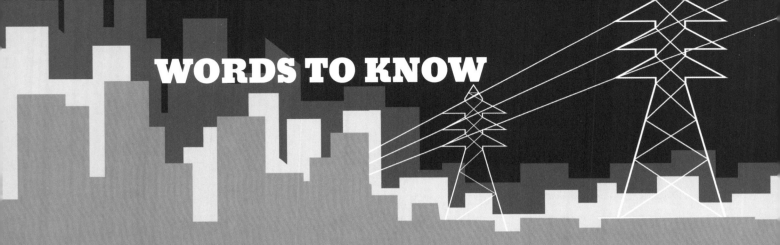

WORDS TO KNOW

circuit—A complete path for electricity to flow.

electricity—A form of energy made by the flow of particles.

electron—A particle with a negative charge of electric energy.

fossil fuel—A form of energy that comes from beneath the earth.

generator—A machine that changes mechanical energy into electric energy.

network—A group or system of things that are connected to each other.

particle—A very small piece of something.

power grid—A network that delivers electricity.

proton—A particle with a positive charge of electric energy.

transformer—A device that reduces or increases electrical voltage.

voltage—The force with which electrons flow.

CONTENTS

From watching TV to charging phones, we rely on electricity for many of our daily tasks.

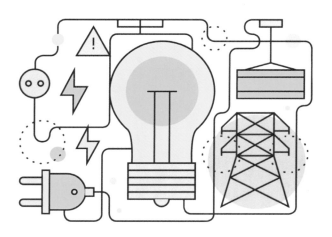

The Importance of Power

What do you need to heat and light your home? What do you need to charge your computer or cell phone? How do you keep foods in your kitchen cool and then heat them in the oven? The answer to all of these questions? Electricity!

Today, we cannot do much without electricity. Electricity powers everything from our televisions to our car radios. We flip a switch when we enter a room, and electricity gives us light.

Why Do We Have Power Grids?

Getting large amounts of electricity to cities and towns takes a lot of planning. Power grids move electricity from where it is made to where it will be used. They are connected to each other in networks.

The first power grid with paying customers was started by Thomas Edison in 1882. He connected several offices in New York City with electrical lighting. The lighting was a new invention at the time.

Engineers plan how electric energy moves from a factory to the people who use it.

Engineers plan and build electric power grids. We use the grid for more than just light and heat. We use it for all forms of communication, from the internet to the telephones that send signals over wires. How have you used electricity today?

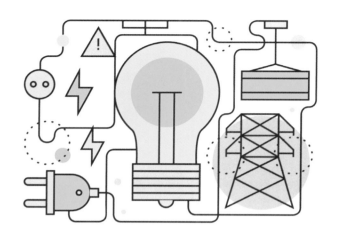

Follow the Power Path

Electricity is the flow of energy from one place to another. It happens in the form of tiny particles called electrons and protons. In current electricity, the electrons and protons flow in a path called a circuit. The flow of electricity starts at a power source, like a battery. Then it flows through the circuit, such as a copper wire. At the end of the circuit is a lightbulb or other electric

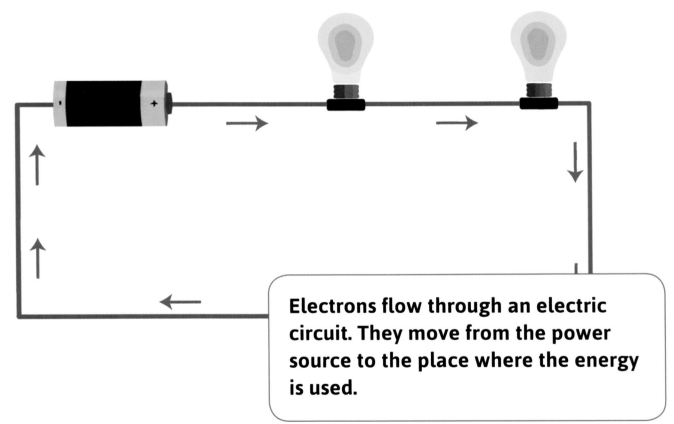

Electrons flow through an electric circuit. They move from the power source to the place where the energy is used.

item that will work when the electrons and protons reach it. When you turn on a light switch, you are seeing current electricity at work.

Making and Moving Electricity

But how does this electricity flow to all of the lights, appliances, and electronics in one house? How do we make such large amounts of electricity? It all starts at large factories called power plants. That is where other energy sources are changed to electrical energy. The energy source might be water, wind, or natural gas. It might be a fossil fuel such as coal.

When the electricity is made, it is not at the right power level to send directly to people's homes and

At a power plant, energy is changed into electricity.

businesses. So the next step is for the electricity to be sent to a device called a transformer, which increases the force at which electrons move. This force is called voltage. Increasing the voltage means more electricity can be moved at once.

One power plant can generate enough electricity to supply hundreds of thousands of homes.

Making Electricity Safe

Once the voltage is increased at a transformer, it can be moved over long electrical wires. This carries it long distances. When the electricity gets close to the places where it will be used, it goes to another transformer. This transformer makes the voltage

Transformers near a power plant increase voltage before sending the electricity throughout the grid system.

lower so it can be sent to homes safely.

After the electricity moves from the transformers, it moves through electrical wires and into homes and businesses. Before entering homes and other buildings, the electrical power is reduced even more. Small transformers on top of electrical poles bring the power down to safer levels.

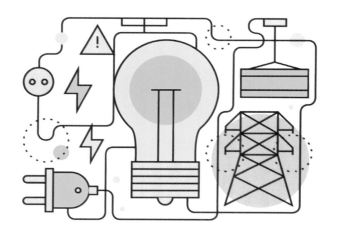

Building Power Grids

Building power grids takes a lot of work by scientists and engineers. Power plants and generators must be large enough to meet the needs of the area they serve. There are three major power grids in the United States. The grids bring power to hundreds of millions of people at their work, homes, and schools.

Keeping the power grids active and working can be difficult. If a transformer breaks down, millions of people could be without power. If a transformer does not change the voltage going through it correctly, people could be in danger. Electricity can be dangerous if it is not moved correctly.

Sometimes power grids fail. This photo shows New York City during a massive blackout.

The Power Business

Communication between power plants is also

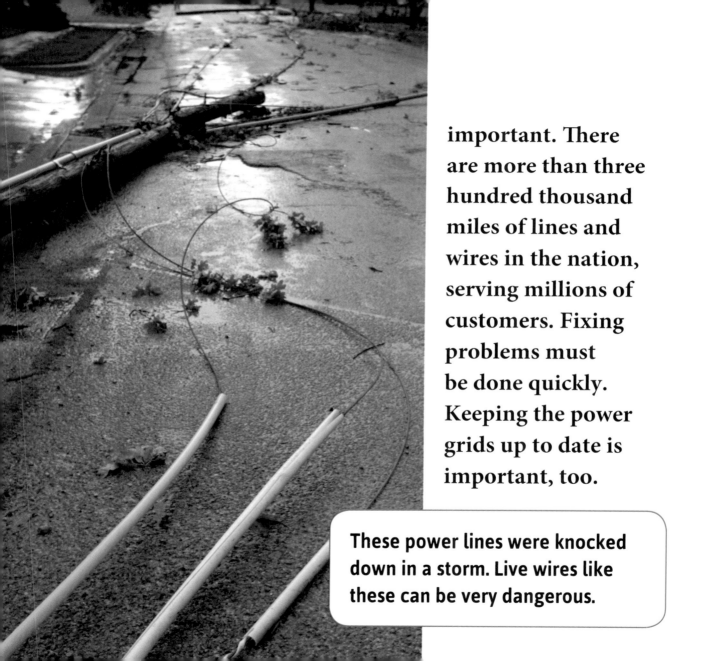

important. There are more than three hundred thousand miles of lines and wires in the nation, serving millions of customers. Fixing problems must be done quickly. Keeping the power grids up to date is important, too.

These power lines were knocked down in a storm. Live wires like these can be very dangerous.

The grid system has been in use since the beginning of the twentieth century. Since that time, the grids have grown. They have been connected. Sections have been updated. At the same time, power companies try to keep the costs low enough for customers to afford electricity. Their workers try not to break the service as they make repairs.

Power lines found on the ground should never be touched. They may be "live" wires, which means they may have electricity running through them.

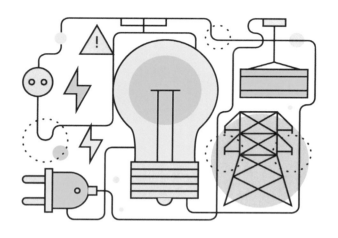

Power of the Future

The power grid system in the United States is aging. Our need for electricity is increasing. This is partly because of how much we use computers, the internet, and other new technologies. There are more people today and more cities and towns to serve. The power grid must keep up with these changes. One way to do this is to create new technologies.

Fossil fuel formed in the earth's surface millions of years ago. Supplies will one day run out. Energy from wind, water, and the sun will not run out.

The "smart grid" is an example of a new technology for the power grid. It uses newer computer technologies to control the grid system. This type of system can help save energy where it is not needed. It can help find places where there is a power outage and fix the problem.

New Power Sources

Many power plants are also trying to find more ways to use renewable resources to make electricity.

That may mean using the energy of the wind, sunlight, or flowing water instead of fossil fuels. Changing to renewable energy will help the environment. It will help save resources for our future. Engineers are working now to improve and build a power grid that will meet our energy needs in the future.

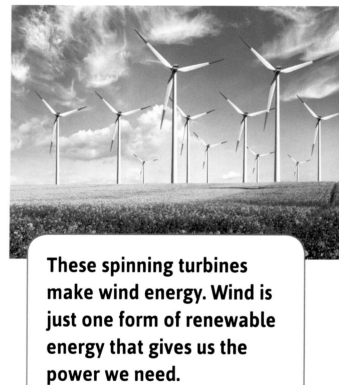

These spinning turbines make wind energy. Wind is just one form of renewable energy that gives us the power we need.

ACTIVITY
ON THE GRID

As you learned in this book, power comes from many sources. Electricity made at a power plant can come from coal, gas, water, or wind. Then it is moved along a path until it finally arrives at homes, schools, or businesses.

- Look at the picture on page 23. It shows one example of an electrical grid. It includes things and places that make electricity and things and places that use electricity.
- Using the list below the picture to guide you, see how many of each you can spot. Do some online research if you're not sure what something is.
- As a follow-up, choose one item from the grid. Write an explanation of how it uses or makes electricity. How does it fit into the grid?

power plant

wind farm

solar farm

pylons

high voltage lines

substations

electric vehicles

farm

city

homes

LEARN MORE

Books

Friedman, Lauri S. *Energy Alternatives*. Farmington Hills, MI: Greenhaven Press, 2011.

Roland, James. *How Circuits Work*. Minneapolis, MN: Lerner, 2017.

Van Vleet, Carmella. *Explore Electricity! With 25 Great Projects*. Chicago, IL: Nomad Press, 2013.

Websites

Energy Kids: U.S. Energy Information Administration
www.eia.gov/kids
Explains about energy history, use, and conservation and provides games and activities.

National Grid: Energy Explorer
www.ngridenergyworld.com
Explores how to use electrical energy safely and efficiently while protecting the environment.

INDEX

Published in 2018 by Enslow Publishing, LLC.
101 W. 23rd Street, Suite 240, New York, NY 10011

Copyright © 2018 by Enslow Publishing, LLC.
All rights reserved.

No part of this book may be reproduced by any means without the written permission of the publisher.

Library of Congress Cataloging-in-Publication Data

Names: Furgang, Kathy, author.
Title: Zoom in on power grids / Kathy Furgang.
Description: New York : Enslow Publishing, 2018. | Series: Zoom in on engineering | Includes bibliographical references and index.
Identifiers: LCCN 2017003015 | ISBN 9780766087071 (library-bound) | ISBN 9780766088399 (pbk.) | ISBN 9780766088337 (6-pack)
Subjects: LCSH: Electric power distribution—Juvenile literature.
Classification: LCC TK3001 .F87 2018 | DDC 621.31—dc23
LC record available at https://lccn.loc.gov/2017003015

Printed in the United States of America

To Our Readers: We have done our best to make sure all website addresses in this book were active and appropriate when we went to press. However, the author and the publisher have no control over and assume no liability for the material available on those websites or on any websites they may link to. Any comments or suggestions can be sent by email to customerservice@enslow.com.

Photo Credits: Cover, p. 1 (inset) Apinan/Shutterstock.com; cover, p. 1 (background) ESB Professional/Shutterstock.com; pp. 5, 9, 15, 19 Bloomicon/Shutterstock.com; pp. 2, 3, 22, 23 (background) Michael Melnikoff/Shutterstock.com; p. 4 ONOKY Photononstop/Alamy Stock Photo; p. 7 michaeljung/Shutterstock.com; p. 10 ducu59us/Shutterstock.com; p. 12 Ron_Thomas/E+/Getty Images; p. 14 Arsentyev Vladimir/Shutterstock.com; p. 16 Bob Gomel/The LIFE Picture Collection/Getty Images; p. 17 Fort Worth Star-Telegram/Tribune News Service/Getty Images; p. 21 Maria Wachala/Moment/Getty Images; p. 23 mathisworks/DigitalVision Vectors/Getty Images; graphic elements (electric lines) Ganibal/Shutterstock.com.